D0343090

DUELING LEGENDS
OFFICIAL HANDBOOK

WRITTEN BY
MICHAEL ANTHONY STEELE AND ARTHUR "SAM" MURAKAMI

SCHOLASTIC INC.

New York   Toronto   London   Auckland   Sydney
Mexico City   New Delhi   Hong Kong   Buenos Aires

© 1996 Kazuki Takahashi
All rights reserved. Published by Scholastic Inc.
SCHOLASTIC and associated logos are trademarks and/or registered trademarks of Scholastic Inc.

ISBN 0-439-76034-8
12 11 10 9 8 7 6 5 4 3 2 1   5 6 7 8 9 10/0
Printed in the U.S.A.
First printing, September 2005

Yugi and his friends love playing the hottest trading card game in the world—Duel Monsters! Duelists compete by pitting mystical creatures, powerful spells, and treacherous traps against each other in awesome, exciting duels!

But there's more to this card game than it seems. . . .

For long ago, when the pyramids were still young, ancient Egyptian leaders and sorcerers played a magical game that pitted ferocious monsters and brutal spells against each other. These shadow games were more than just a pastime—they became part of a ceremonial ritual that predicted the future and foresaw one's destiny.

However, with so much magic and monsters in the world, it wasn't long before the powerful shadow games spun out of control and brought the Egyptian civilization to the edge of destruction. Fortunately, their brave pharaoh stepped in and averted disaster with the help of the seven magical artifacts known as the Millennium Items.

Now, in present times, the shadow games have been revived in the form of the modern trading card game Duel Monsters. But lucky for us, these monsters are just images on cards. They're not real.

Or are they?

It's time to duel!

YUGI MUTO

Yugi is a shy student at Domino High School who loves to play Duel Monsters. But by being shy, he's also a loner. All he has ever wanted is a friend. Little does he know that he will soon encounter the greatest friend of all. . . .

One day, Yugi's Grandpa gives him a mysterious Egyptian artifact called the Millennium Puzzle. No one in history has ever been able to solve the puzzle, but after much persistence, Yugi solves it, and something amazing happens! He is infused with the imprisoned spirit of an Egyptian Pharaoh, giving Yugi incredible powers and creating his alter ego, Yami Yugi!

Yugi has had many formidable ordeals in his dueling legacy. First, he had to win the Duelist Kingdom tournament to rescue his Grandpa's soul from the clutches of Pegasus. Before you can say "It's time to duel," Yugi was competing in the Battle City Tournament to save the world from Marik! Then Yugi had to help Kaiba stop Kaiba's stepfather, Gozaburo, from ruling the world through virtual reality! Most recently, Yugi had to rescue Earth from Dartz when Dartz revived the Grand Dragon Leviathan, a huge behemoth that destroyed Atlantis! Yugi's job is never done!

GRANDPA

Yugi's grandfather is an expert on games from all over the world. He owns the neighborhood gaming shop and is especially well versed in the ways of Duel Monsters. In fact, he is the one who originally teaches Yugi how to play. He not only teaches him the rules, but he also teaches him to play with honor and about the "heart of the cards" — believe in yourself and your deck and anything can happen!

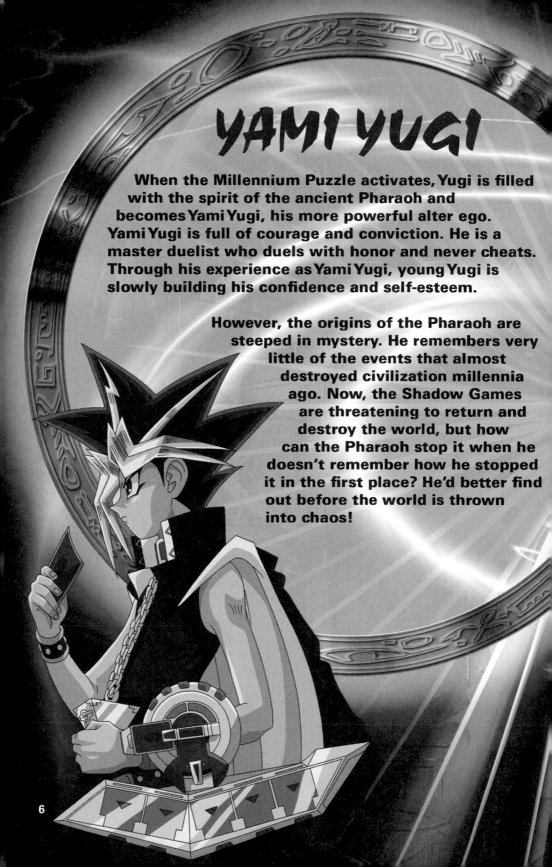

YAMI YUGI

When the Millennium Puzzle activates, Yugi is filled with the spirit of the ancient Pharaoh and becomes Yami Yugi, his more powerful alter ego. Yami Yugi is full of courage and conviction. He is a master duelist who duels with honor and never cheats. Through his experience as Yami Yugi, young Yugi is slowly building his confidence and self-esteem.

However, the origins of the Pharaoh are steeped in mystery. He remembers very little of the events that almost destroyed civilization millennia ago. Now, the Shadow Games are threatening to return and destroy the world, but how can the Pharaoh stop it when he doesn't remember how he stopped it in the first place? He'd better find out before the world is thrown into chaos!

YUGI'S MONSTERS

Yugi has collected a host of fierce and diverse monsters. Although some are mightier than others, the true power of Yugi's collection doesn't lie in the monsters themselves but in how he plays them. Yugi's belief in his deck's abilities is one of his keys to victory.

DARK MAGICIAN GIRL

Although she's the apprentice to the Dark Magician, her spells are not to be taken lightly. When her fellow spellcasters fall in battle, she becomes stronger and even more determined!

Recently, Dark Magician Girl sought Yugi's help in rescuing both Earth and the entire Realm of Monsters from destruction by Dartz and his Grand Dragon Leviathan!

DARK MAGICIAN

Yugi's favorite and most trusted monster, the Dark Magician doesn't pull rabbits out of hats. He unleashes powerful Dark Magic Attack to destroy enemies.

MAGICIAN OF BLACK CHAOS

Summoned from chaotic energies, Magician of Black Chaos has faced the toughest of enemies! But with the help of two other magicians — Dark Magician and Dark Magician Girl — he has taken down numerous powerful duelists, including Pegasus!

DARK SAGE

The Dark Magician undergoes thousands of years of training to perfect his dark powers and transform into the wizened Dark Sage!

MONSTER QUESTION # 1

WHICH MONSTER THAT ODION SUMMONED IS ALSO A TRAP? • • • • • • • • • •

VALKYRION THE MAGNA WARRIOR

Three magnet warriors, Alpha, Beta, and Gamma, combine to form the mighty Valkyrion the Magna Warrior, making this a very "attractive" monster.

ALPHA THE MAGNET WARRIOR

This warrior strikes with a powerful sword to pulverize its foes into particles!

DUELING LEGEND QUESTION # 1

WHICH DUELING DUO SPEAKS IN RHYME?

BETA THE MAGNET WARRIOR

Don't underestimate Beta the Magnet Warrior because of its cute appearance — this minute monster packs a powerful wallop!

GAMMA THE MAGNET WARRIOR

When combined with Alpha and Beta, Gamma's wings give Valkyrion the advantage of flight.

WHO RIDES HIS OWN KILLER WHALE INTO BATTLE? • • • • • • • • • •

WINGED DRAGON, GUARDIAN OF THE FORTRESS #1

This dragon shoots out flaming fireballs to light up the darkness and burn enemies to a crisp!

MAMMOTH GRAVEYARD

The ground shakes but its bones never rattle as he charges at his opponents!

B. SKULL DRAGON

This massive monster is created by the power of teamwork — B. Skull Dragon is a fusion of Yugi's Summoned Skull and Joey's Red-Eyes B. Dragon. By working together, Yugi and Joey summoned this battling beast and took down the Paradox Brothers!

DUELING LEGEND QUESTION # 2

WHICH DUELIST IS ALSO A REAL MAGICIAN?

SUMMONED SKULL

This ghastly creature's primary weapon is a brutal electric shock! During Duelist Kingdom, Yugi used Summoned Skull to give Weevil's Great Moth the shock of its life!

CHIMERA THE FLYING MYTHICAL BEAST

Gazelle the King of Mythical Beasts and Berfomet fuse together to form this fabled creature. However, it is quite real and very dangerous.

13

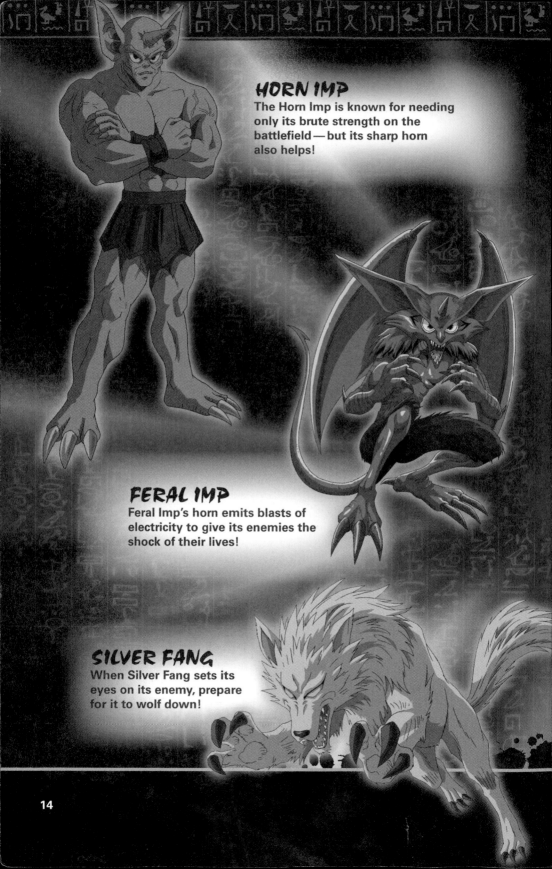

HORN IMP

The Horn Imp is known for needing only its brute strength on the battlefield — but its sharp horn also helps!

FERAL IMP

Feral Imp's horn emits blasts of electricity to give its enemies the shock of their lives!

SILVER FANG

When Silver Fang sets its eyes on its enemy, prepare for it to wolf down!

BERFOMET

How does a flying beast with four arms grab you? Any way it wants!

BIG SHIELD GARDNA

This warrior will not falter from protecting Yugi against vicious attacks with his enormous shield!

EXODIA THE FORBIDDEN ONE

When all five pieces of Exodia are gathered, Exodia the Forbidden One emerges to obliterate its opponent instantly! In Yugi and Kaiba's first-ever duel, Yugi summoned Exodia the Forbidden One to defeat Kaiba! Unfortunately, Yugi was never able to summon Exodia the Forbidden One again after Weevil threw Yugi's Exodia card into the ocean when they sailed to Duelist Kingdom.

GIANT SOLDIER OF STONE

This giant dwarfs most adversaries on the battlefield and easily swats away weak attacks with its pair of twin stone swords!

DUELING LEGEND QUESTION # 3

WHO INVENTED THE DUEL DISK?

SHONEN JUMP'S Yu-Gi-Oh!

DUELING LEGENDS
OFFICIAL HANDBOOK

WRITTEN BY
MICHAEL ANTHONY STEELE AND ARTHUR "SAM" MURAKAMI

SCHOLASTIC INC.

New York   Toronto   London   Auckland   Sydney
Mexico City   New Delhi   Hong Kong   Buenos Aires

ISBN 0-439-76034-8
12 11 10 9 8 7 6 5 4 3 2 1   5 6 7 8 9 10/0
Printed in the U.S.A.
First printing, September 2005

YUGI AND HIS FRIENDS LOVE PLAYING THE HOTTEST TRADING CARD GAME IN THE WORLD—DUEL MONSTERS! DUELISTS COMPETE BY PITTING MYSTICAL CREATURES, POWERFUL SPELLS, AND TREACHEROUS TRAPS AGAINST EACH OTHER IN AWESOME, EXCITING DUELS!

BUT THERE'S MORE TO THIS CARD GAME THAN IT SEEMS. . . .

FOR LONG AGO, WHEN THE PYRAMIDS WERE STILL YOUNG, ANCIENT EGYPTIAN LEADERS AND SORCERERS PLAYED A MAGICAL GAME THAT PITTED FEROCIOUS MONSTERS AND BRUTAL SPELLS AGAINST EACH OTHER. THESE SHADOW GAMES WERE MORE THAN JUST A PASTIME—THEY BECAME PART OF A CEREMONIAL RITUAL THAT PREDICTED THE FUTURE AND FORESAW ONE'S DESTINY.

HOWEVER, WITH SO MUCH MAGIC AND MONSTERS IN THE WORLD, IT WASN'T LONG BEFORE THE POWERFUL SHADOW GAMES SPUN OUT OF CONTROL AND BROUGHT THE EGYPTIAN CIVILIZATION TO THE EDGE OF DESTRUCTION. FORTUNATELY, THEIR BRAVE PHARAOH STEPPED IN AND AVERTED DISASTER WITH THE HELP OF THE SEVEN MAGICAL ARTIFACTS KNOWN AS THE MILLENNIUM ITEMS.

NOW, IN PRESENT TIMES, THE SHADOW GAMES HAVE BEEN REVIVED IN THE FORM OF THE MODERN TRADING CARD GAME DUEL MONSTERS. BUT LUCKY FOR US, THESE MONSTERS ARE JUST IMAGES ON CARDS. THEY'RE NOT REAL.

OR ARE THEY?

It's time to duel!

YUGI MUTO

Yugi is a shy student at Domino High School who loves to play Duel Monsters. But by being shy, he's also a loner. All he has ever wanted is a friend. Little does he know that he will soon encounter the greatest friend of all. . . .

One day, Yugi's Grandpa gives him a mysterious Egyptian artifact called the Millennium Puzzle. No one in history has ever been able to solve the puzzle, but after much persistence, Yugi solves it, and something amazing happens! He is infused with the imprisoned spirit of an Egyptian Pharaoh, giving Yugi incredible powers and creating his alter ego, Yami Yugi!

Yugi has had many formidable ordeals in his dueling legacy. First, he had to win the Duelist Kingdom tournament to rescue his Grandpa's soul from the clutches of Pegasus. Before you can say "It's time to duel," Yugi was competing in the Battle City Tournament to save the world from Marik! Then Yugi had to help Kaiba stop Kaiba's stepfather, Gozaburo, from ruling the world through virtual reality! Most recently, Yugi had to rescue Earth from Dartz when Dartz revived the Grand Dragon Leviathan, a huge behemoth that destroyed Atlantis! Yugi's job is never done!

GRANDPA

Yugi's grandfather is an expert on games from all over the world. He owns the neighborhood gaming shop and is especially well versed in the ways of Duel Monsters. In fact, he is the one who originally teaches Yugi how to play. He not only teaches him the rules, but he also teaches him to play with honor and about the "heart of the cards" — believe in yourself and your deck and anything can happen!

5

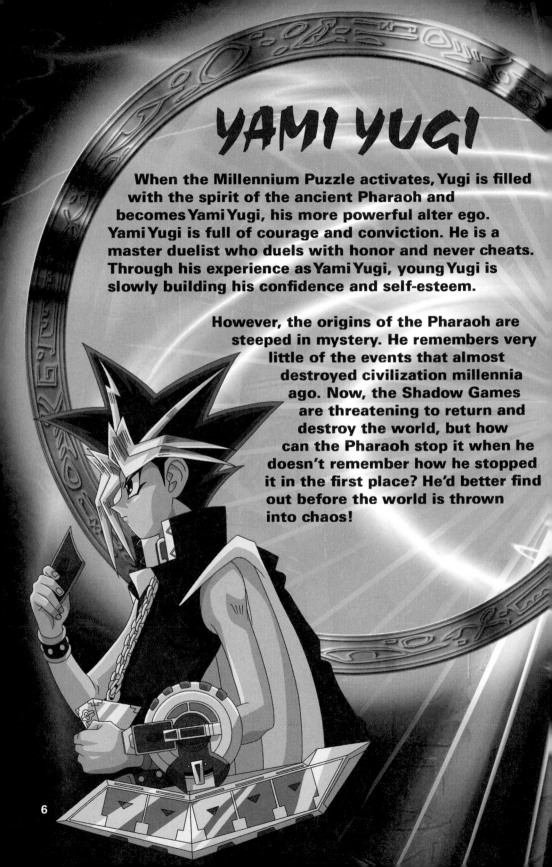

YAMI YUGI

When the Millennium Puzzle activates, Yugi is filled with the spirit of the ancient Pharaoh and becomes Yami Yugi, his more powerful alter ego. Yami Yugi is full of courage and conviction. He is a master duelist who duels with honor and never cheats. Through his experience as Yami Yugi, young Yugi is slowly building his confidence and self-esteem.

However, the origins of the Pharaoh are steeped in mystery. He remembers very little of the events that almost destroyed civilization millennia ago. Now, the Shadow Games are threatening to return and destroy the world, but how can the Pharaoh stop it when he doesn't remember how he stopped it in the first place? He'd better find out before the world is thrown into chaos!

YUGI'S MONSTERS

Yugi has collected a host of fierce and diverse monsters. Although some are mightier than others, the true power of Yugi's collection doesn't lie in the monsters themselves but in how he plays them. Yugi's belief in his deck's abilities is one of his keys to victory.

DARK MAGICIAN GIRL

Although she's the apprentice to the Dark Magician, her spells are not to be taken lightly. When her fellow spellcasters fall in battle, she becomes stronger and even more determined!

Recently, Dark Magician Girl sought Yugi's help in rescuing both Earth and the entire Realm of Monsters from destruction by Dartz and his Grand Dragon Leviathan!

DARK MAGICIAN

Yugi's favorite and most trusted monster, the Dark Magician doesn't pull rabbits out of hats. He unleashes powerful Dark Magic Attack to destroy enemies.

MAGICIAN OF BLACK CHAOS

Summoned from chaotic energies, Magician of Black Chaos has faced the toughest of enemies! But with the help of two other magicians—Dark Magician and Dark Magician Girl—he has taken down numerous powerful duelists, including Pegasus!

DARK SAGE

The Dark Magician undergoes thousands of years of training to perfect his dark powers and transform into the wizened Dark Sage!

VALKYRION THE MAGNA WARRIOR

Three magnet warriors, Alpha, Beta, and Gamma, combine to form the mighty Valkyrion the Magna Warrior, making this a very "attractive" monster.

ALPHA THE MAGNET WARRIOR

This warrior strikes with a powerful sword to pulverize its foes into particles!

DUELING LEGEND QUESTION # 1

WHICH DUELING DUO SPEAKS IN RHYME?

BETA THE MAGNET WARRIOR

Don't underestimate Beta the Magnet Warrior because of its cute appearance—this minute monster packs a powerful wallop!

GAMMA THE MAGNET WARRIOR

When combined with Alpha and Beta, Gamma's wings give Valkyrion the advantage of flight.

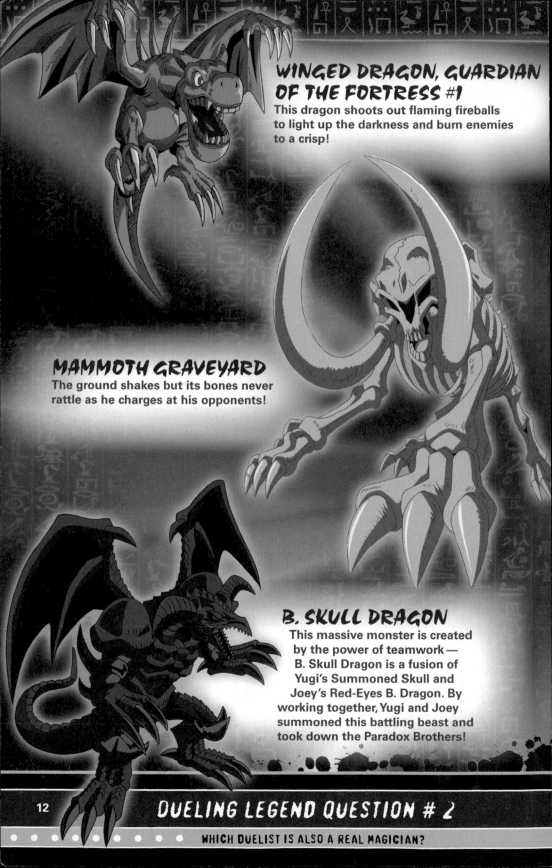

WINGED DRAGON, GUARDIAN OF THE FORTRESS #1

This dragon shoots out flaming fireballs to light up the darkness and burn enemies to a crisp!

MAMMOTH GRAVEYARD

The ground shakes but its bones never rattle as he charges at his opponents!

B. SKULL DRAGON

This massive monster is created by the power of teamwork — B. Skull Dragon is a fusion of Yugi's Summoned Skull and Joey's Red-Eyes B. Dragon. By working together, Yugi and Joey summoned this battling beast and took down the Paradox Brothers!

DUELING LEGEND QUESTION # 2

WHICH DUELIST IS ALSO A REAL MAGICIAN?

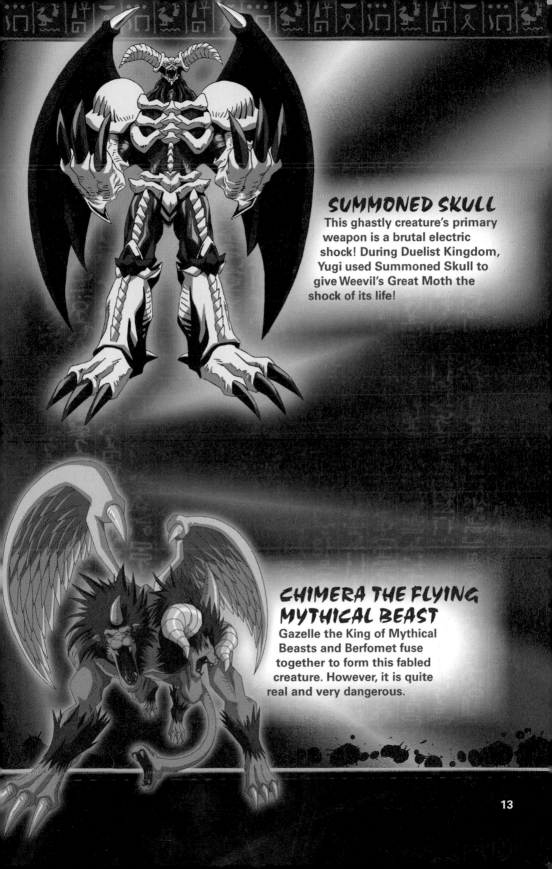

SUMMONED SKULL

This ghastly creature's primary weapon is a brutal electric shock! During Duelist Kingdom, Yugi used Summoned Skull to give Weevil's Great Moth the shock of its life!

CHIMERA THE FLYING MYTHICAL BEAST

Gazelle the King of Mythical Beasts and Berfomet fuse together to form this fabled creature. However, it is quite real and very dangerous.

HORN IMP

The Horn Imp is known for needing only its brute strength on the battlefield—but its sharp horn also helps!

FERAL IMP

Feral Imp's horn emits blasts of electricity to give its enemies the shock of their lives!

SILVER FANG

When Silver Fang sets its eyes on its enemy, prepare for it to wolf down!

BERFOMET
How does a flying beast with four arms grab you? Any way it wants!

BIG SHIELD GARDNA
This warrior will not falter from protecting Yugi against vicious attacks with his enormous shield!

MONSTER QUESTION # 3

15

WHICH EGYPTIAN GOD CARD DID ISHIZU GIVE KAIBA? ● ● ● ● ● ● ● ● ● ●

EXODIA THE FORBIDDEN ONE

When all five pieces of Exodia are gathered, Exodia the Forbidden One emerges to obliterate its opponent instantly! In Yugi and Kaiba's first-ever duel, Yugi summoned Exodia the Forbidden One to defeat Kaiba! Unfortunately, Yugi was never able to summon Exodia the Forbidden One again after Weevil threw Yugi's Exodia card into the ocean when they sailed to Duelist Kingdom.

GIANT SOLDIER OF STONE

This giant dwarfs most adversaries on the battlefield and easily swats away weak attacks with its pair of twin stone swords!

DUELING LEGEND QUESTION # 3

WHO INVENTED THE DUEL DISK?

JINZO
Not only does Jinzo destroy enemies with its powerful Cyber Energy Shock, its laserlike gaze spots all its opponents' traps and demolishes them!

GILFORD THE LIGHTNING
With a special lightning blast from Gilford the Lightning's sword, he instantly sends the opponent's monsters straight to the graveyard before they even know it!

TÉA GARDNER

Aspiring dancer Téa, among all of Yugi's companions, is often the voice of reason. She is the biggest supporter in the group and is always there to cheer everyone on. She never stops encouraging her friends to believe in themselves and to never give up. Even though she isn't a duelist, Téa has proven many times that she's willing to duel to help her friends and has taken on formidable opponents, such as Mai and The Big 5!

TRISTAN TAYLOR

Tristan doesn't duel much, but he likes to support his friends Joey and Yugi as they battle against their opponents. Whenever Yugi is on an adventure to save the world, Tristan is always there giving 110% of his support. Although he and Joey are good friends, they often bicker and get on each other's nerves with comical results. In the end, however, they always cover each other's backs when things get tough. Tristan is willing to do whatever it takes to support and cheer on his friends.

Mai Valentine

Mai is as dangerous as she is pretty, making her very dangerous! In the beginning, she was aloof and only dueled for riches and fame, but she learned the value of friendship and honor from Yugi and Joey, making her a valuable ally.

However, she recently joined up with Dartz to defeat Yugi and his friends to prove that she's a great duelist on her own! Will she be able to face her inner demons and learn the true importance of dueling and friendship?

WHICH MONSTER'S TRUE POWER CAN BE UNLEASHED IF YOU CAN READ ANCIENT EGYPTIAN WRITING? •

MAI'S MONSTERS

Mai's collection of monsters reflects Mai herself — dangerous women!

HARPIE LADY SISTERS

These three mythical creatures become very real on the dueling field. They often fight as one, leaving opponents little choice but to surrender.

DUELING LEGEND QUESTION # 8

WHO POSSESSES THE MILLENNIUM EYE?

HARPIES' PET DRAGON

The Harpie Lady Sisters' pet is far from cute and cuddly. The only tricks this pet knows are crush, slash, and destroy!

AMAZONESS CHAIN MASTER

Amazonesses are some of the most formidable warriors in the world. This one extends her powerful strike with a long spiked chain!

37

AMAZONESS SWORDSWOMAN

A finely honed blade is the weapon of choice for this Amazoness.

AMAZONESS FIGHTER

This fighter uses her Amazonian strength as her only weapon. Then again, that's all she needs.

Yami Bakura

The Millennium Ring has the power to detect other Millennium Items, putting him constantly into conflict with others who wield Millennium Items. The spirit wants to get all seven Millennium Items, but what does he want it for, and who exactly is this spirit?

BAKURA AND HIS MONSTERS

Bakura is a good friend of Yugi and pals . . . but he hides a dangerous secret. Bakura has the Millennium Ring — and the evil spirit that resides within it! When the evil spirit takes over, Bakura's personality totally changes from the nicest guy to the scariest villain!

SEVEN-ARMED FIEND

With seven arms, this beast needs no weapons to challenge other monsters!

PUPPET MASTER

The vile creature pulls all the right strings to come out on top.

DARK NECROFEAR

A dark and powerful spirit, she brings you nightmares that are scarier-looking than the doll in her arms!

DUELING LEGEND QUESTION # 9

WHO IS THE MOST INSECT-RIDDEN DUELIST?

Seto Kaiba

Seto Kaiba is the wealthy CEO of KaibaCorp—a multinational high-tech corporation he took over from his stepfather, Gozaburo Kaiba. As the inventor of the Duel Disk, he makes it very clear that his real passion is Duel Monsters. He is one of the best duelists in the world, making him Yugi's greatest rival. On the dueling field, he truly believes he can defeat all who challenge him.

Kaiba is a master duelist who believes that trading card gaming is all about power. However, despite his rough exterior, Kaiba is very loyal and cares about the kids of the world, especially his younger brother, Mokuba. The two Kaiba brothers lived in an orphanage, so he understands how hard it is for children to find happiness. Therefore, Kaiba's dream is to create Kaiba Land amusement parks for children all around the world.

MOKUBA KAIBA

Mokuba loves his older brother very much, but he is also friends with Yugi and his pals. Unlike his brother, he is willing to ask them for help when he or Seto is in trouble. He's also a whiz kid who knows the ins and outs of computers like the back of his hand.

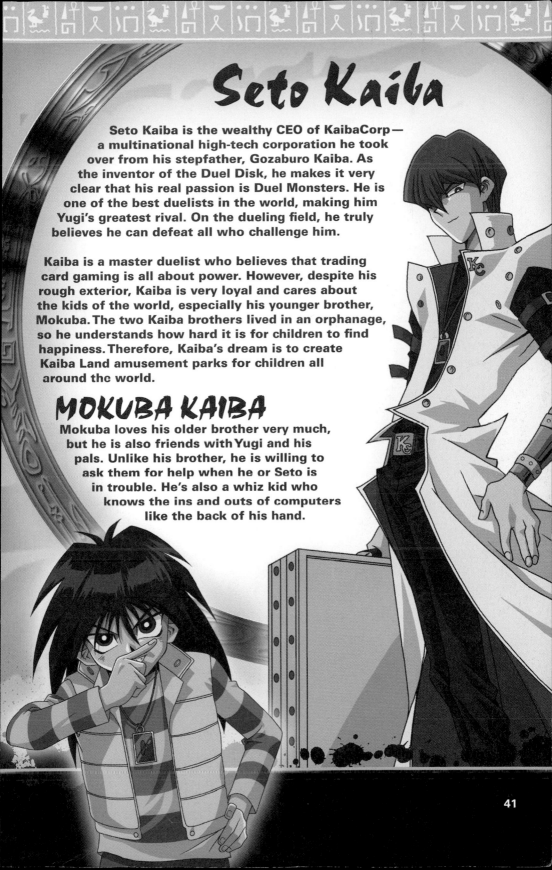

KAIBA'S MONSTERS

Kaiba prides himself on collecting the most powerful monsters in the world so that he can accomplish his goal of defeating Yugi and regaining his title as a champion duelist. He's just as ruthless a duelist as he is brutal in the business world, so he usually gets what he wants.

BLUE-EYES WHITE DRAGON

If one monster represents Kaiba, it's Blue-Eyes White Dragon, one of the most powerful dragons in all of Duel Monsters. Only three Blue-Eyes exist in the world, and Kaiba owns all three!

BLUE-EYES ULTIMATE DRAGON

If you thought one Blue-Eyes White Dragon was scary, then your fright is tripled when three Blue-Eyes White Dragons fuse together to form Blue-Eyes Ultimate Dragon! This proves three heads are better than one!

DUELING LEGEND QUESTION # 10

WHO POSSESSES THE MILLENNIUM ROD?

LA JINN THE MYSTICAL GENIE OF THE LAMP

This genie doesn't grant wishes . . . unless your wish is to be beaten on the dueling field!

HITOTSU-ME GIANT

Him giant! Him very strong! Him smash other monsters to bits!

SAGGI THE DARK CLOWN

When it's time to send in this clown, the only show to see is one of might, magic, and dark illusions!

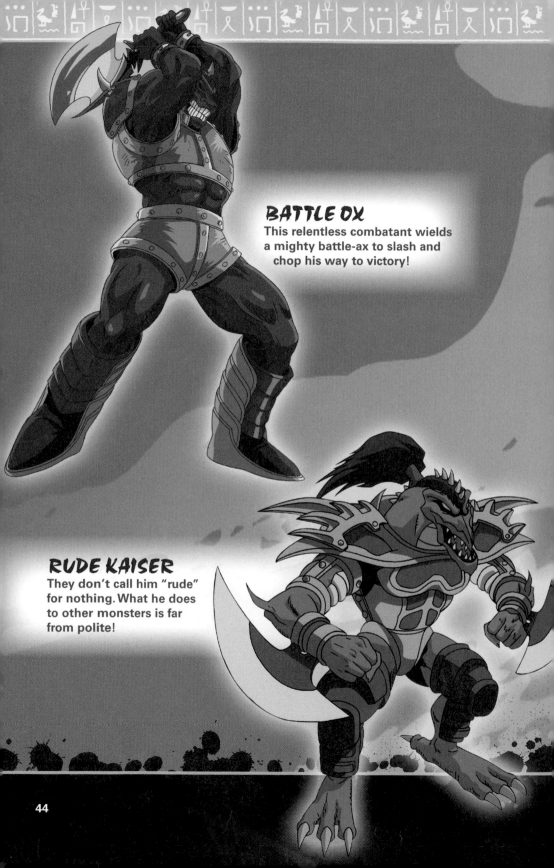

BATTLE OX
This relentless combatant wields a mighty battle-ax to slash and chop his way to victory!

RUDE KAISER
They don't call him "rude" for nothing. What he does to other monsters is far from polite!

JUDGE MAN

When he swings his spiked maces, this judge finds everyone guilty!

RABID HORSEMAN

As a fusion of Battle Ox and Mystic Horseman, Rabid Horseman wields a mighty battle-ax and gallops onto the field with ruthless determination!

SWORDSTALKER

A wicked grin stretches across this creature's face as he steps onto the field with his razor-sharp blade.

VORSE RAIDER

This warrior is feared for his relentless fighting style and double-bladed staff.

BLADE KNIGHT

With shield and long sword in hand, this knight crusades into battle and shows no mercy! Kaiba unleashed this monster for the first time during the Battle City Tournament four-way battle royal at the Duel Tower with stunning results!

DUELING LEGEND QUESTION # 11

WHO DUELED TO HELP PAY FOR HIS SISTER'S EYE OPERATION?

X-HEAD CANNON
Both its spiked torso and dual cannons send fear down the spines of this robot's enemies!

Y-DRAGON HEAD
This robotic dragon is just as deadly as the real thing. It soars into battle blasting balls of fire!

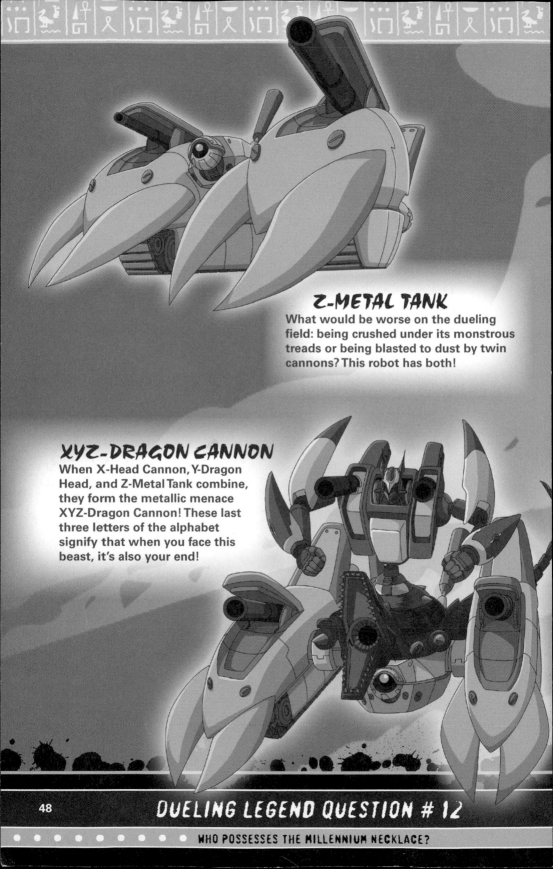

Z-METAL TANK

What would be worse on the dueling field: being crushed under its monstrous treads or being blasted to dust by twin cannons? This robot has both!

XYZ-DRAGON CANNON

When X-Head Cannon, Y-Dragon Head, and Z-Metal Tank combine, they form the metallic menace XYZ-Dragon Cannon! These last three letters of the alphabet signify that when you face this beast, it's also your end!

DUELING LEGEND QUESTION # 12

WHO POSSESSES THE MILLENNIUM NECKLACE?

Maximillion Pegasus

Through his research into ancient Egyptian games, Maximillion Pegasus has become the creator of the worldwide phenomenon trading card game Duel Monsters. While traveling throughout Egypt, the mysterious Shadi replaces Pegasus's left eye with an ancient artifact called the Millennium Eye, which allows him to read another person's mind. That's especially useful when dueling, for he gets to know what his opponent's strategy is even before he executes it!

Pegasus initiates the Duelist Kingdom Tournament to gather the greatest duelists in the world. By using the magic of the Millennium Items, he may be able to revive his long-lost wife, Cecilia.

With the Millennium Eye and his ability to read the minds of his opponents, he can defeat all who challenge him! Against Yugi, however, this plan fell apart when Yugi switched back and forth from Yugi to Yami Yugi in order to keep one of their thoughts hidden from Pegasus at all times.

PEGASUS'S MONSTERS

Some of Pegasus's monsters may seem innocent and harmless, but never judge a book by its cover. Being a fan of cartoons, Pegasus created the Toon World card and his cadre of Toon Monsters. Turning and flip-flopping and somersaulting, these Toons can dodge almost every attack! Let the fun begin!

TOON SUMMONED SKULL

This Toon version of Summoned Skull may appear cute, but one look into its crazy eyes proves that this monster is not to be trifled with!

TOON MERMAID
This mermaid hides in the safety of her shell while she dishes out a barrage of deadly arrows!

DRAGON PIPER
With its magical flute, Dragon Piper can lull your dragon into submission.

RYU-RAN

Still clinging to his eggshell, this dragon was born with more strength than that of most grown dragons.

MANGA RYU-RAN

This Toon version of Ryu-Ran stomps monsters to dust! It's nothing to laugh at!

PARROT DRAGON

When his beak snaps shut, he tries to snatch more than just a tasty cracker!

BLUE-EYES TOON DRAGON

Toon versions of other monsters have all their power and none of their weaknesses. Kaiba despises Blue-Eyes Toon Dragon for making a mockery of his favorite monster, Blue-Eyes White Dragon.

DARK RABBIT

This rabbit won't invite you to a tea party. It will invite you to your doom!

53

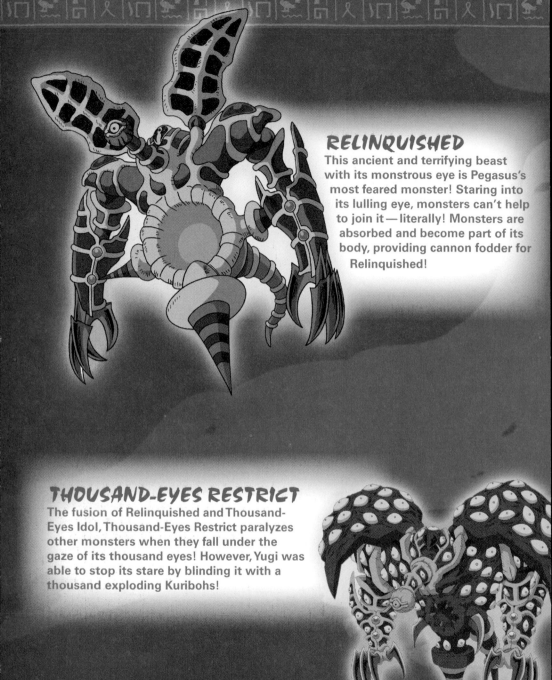

RELINQUISHED

This ancient and terrifying beast with its monstrous eye is Pegasus's most feared monster! Staring into its lulling eye, monsters can't help to join it — literally! Monsters are absorbed and become part of its body, providing cannon fodder for Relinquished!

THOUSAND-EYES RESTRICT

The fusion of Relinquished and Thousand-Eyes Idol, Thousand-Eyes Restrict paralyzes other monsters when they fall under the gaze of its thousand eyes! However, Yugi was able to stop its stare by blinding it with a thousand exploding Kuribohs!

PANIK AND HIS MONSTER

Pegasus hired PaniK to eliminate duelists during the Duelist Kingdom Tournament by winning their Star Chips. This ruthless duelist defeated Mai, but she was able to stay in the tournament when Yugi won her Star Chips back.

CASTLE OF DARK ILLUSIONS

This flying fortress forces opponents to fight enemies hidden in a shroud of darkness.

PARADOX BROTHERS AND THEIR MONSTERS

The dueling duo Paradox Brothers speak in rhyme, but there's no riddle to their skills. These Pegasus henchmen guard the entrance to his castle, and their special dueling field is a labyrinth that confounds Yugi and Joey.

GATE GUARDIAN

Gate Guardian, Paradox Brothers' greatest monster, combines the elements of lightning, water, and wind to attack with severe natural disasters! You don't want to be standing in a pool of water when an electrical blast strikes you!

SHADOW GHOUL

A grotesque beast like this can only lurk in the shadows.

55

WEEVIL UNDERWOOD AND HIS MONSTERS

Weevil Underwood is a pest and a trickster! His web of cards is brimming with burrowing bugs and creepy crawlers. He will often unleash crippling parasites into an opponent's deck.

BASIC INSECT

This monster swoops into battle and cleaves the opposition in two with its jagged scythes!

GREAT MOTH

This moth isn't attracted to light but to fierce combat, emitting poisonous clouds with the flap of its wings! Evolving inside the Cocoon of Evolution, Great Moth is a powerful pest, but if it stays in the cocoon longer, it can evolve into the even more dangerous Perfectly Ultimate Great Moth.

INSECT QUEEN

Weevil's main monster since the Battle City Tournament, this royal ravager not only eats other bugs to become stronger, she lays eggs to increase the infestation, too!

REX RAPTOR AND HIS MONSTERS

Rex Raptor is an intense dinosaur duelist whose deck is packed full of mammoth monsters. Things have been downhill ever since he lost his Red-Eyes B. Dragon to Joey — he lost a lot of fame and respect from the dueling community. Therefore, he joined up with Dartz to try to win his rematch against Joey, but he lost and had his soul captured.

TWO-HEADED KING REX

With two ferocious heads, this dino is double trouble! Watch out for its stamping feet!

SWORD ARM OF DRAGON

It's difficult for most opponents to even get close to this spiked beast when it swings its tail and slices foes in half!

MAKO TSUNAMI AND HIS MONSTERS

Mako Tsunami is a sea duelist whose deck is flooded with underwater monsters. He duels just like the ocean that he loves — fury and the power of pounding waves! Full of pride and honor, he dreams of captaining his own fishing boat — just like his missing father.

THE LEGENDARY FISHERMAN

Mako's very favorite monster, this fisherman rides his own killer whale into battle and skewers everything he sees!

DUELING LEGEND QUESTION # 14

WHO DUELS USING HARPIE LADY?

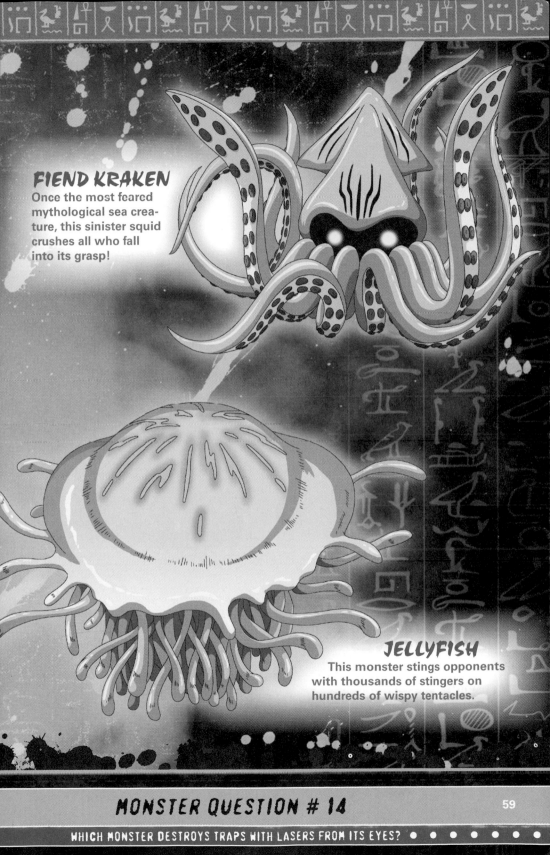

FIEND KRAKEN
Once the most feared mythological sea creature, this sinister squid crushes all who fall into its grasp!

JELLYFISH
This monster stings opponents with thousands of stingers on hundreds of wispy tentacles.

WHICH MONSTER DESTROYS TRAPS WITH LASERS FROM ITS EYES? ● ● ● ● ● ● ●

KAIRYU-SHIN

When this gigantic sea serpent swims near your ship, be prepared to see Davy Jones's locker!

FORTRESS WHALE

With a long horn and turrets on its back, this whale swims into any battle with complete confidence!

DUELING LEGEND QUESTION # 15

WHO ARRANGED THE DUELIST KINGDOM COMPETITION?

BONZ AND HIS MONSTERS

Bonz's eerie deck is swarming with ghouls and zombies.

CRASS CLOWN

This hideous clown is nothing to laugh at!

CLOWN ZOMBIE

Bonz will often summon his monsters back from the graveyard, turning them into gruesome zombies. This is what happens when Crass Clown returns from the dead.

WHICH MONSTER DID YUGI GIVE TO JOEY ON THE BOAT TO DUELIST KINGDOM? • • • • • •

ARMORED ZOMBIE
The battle never ends for this ancient samurai warrior!

DRAGON ZOMBIE
When this dragon returns from the dead, his breath is worse than ever!

PUMPKING THE KING OF GHOSTS
Nightmares are the kingdom of this haunting king! It injects ectoplasm into zombies from its creepy tentacles to power them up!

DUELING LEGEND QUESTION # 16

WHICH DUELIST IS A BIG FAN OF CARTOONS?

BANDIT KEITH AND HIS MONSTERS

His name says it all — Bandit Keith is a cheat and thief! He'll do anything to win, even if it means breaking the rules. He stole Joey's card to enter the Duelist Kingdom finals, but no bad deed goes unpunished, as Pegasus unceremoniously kicked Bandit Keith out of the tournament by dropping him into the ocean! Since that day, only bad things have happened to Bandit Keith — he was hypnotized by Marik and became one of his minions. Remember, cheating doesn't pay!

PENDULUM MACHINE
This nightmarish contraption is ready to slice the competition in half!

SLOT MACHINE
When monsters go up against this Las Vegas reject, they're gambling with their lives!

LAUNCHER SPIDER
The enormous arachnid launches a barrage of explosive missiles against its enemies!

Shadi

Shadi is a mysterious observer who rarely appears before Yugi and pals, but when he does, they know something important is about to happen! His Millennium Key allows him to unlock and enter other people's minds.

MILLENNIUM KEY

MILLENNIUM SCALE

DUELING LEGEND QUESTION # 17

WHO IS MARIK'S ADOPTED BROTHER?

MARIK AND HIS MONSTERS

The nefarious Marik Ishtar leads an entire gang of ruthless Rare Hunters that hunt duelists in order to take their rare cards! By owning lots of rare cards, he can achieve his ultimate goals of destroying the Pharaoh and taking his Millennium Puzzle. Marik has his own Millennium Item — the Millennium Rod. With the Rod, Marik is able to control other people's minds, which helped him greatly when he took control of Yugi's friends Joey and Téa! Not only that, he holds one of the powerful Egyptian God Cards, The Winged Dragon of Ra!

MILLENNIUM ROD

MAKYURA THE DESTRUCTOR

With long sharp claws on its arms, it's slice-and-dice time!

MONSTER QUESTION # 17

WHO CARRIES TWO SHARP LANCES AND RIDES A HORSE INTO BATTLE? ● ● ● ●

LAVA GOLEM

Marik's unusual monster doesn't even stay on his side of the dueling field — Lava Golem goes to the opponent's side! However, Marik's opponent is locked in a cage — under a cascade of burning magma!

DRILLAGO

Drillago is extremely well equipped to drill to the heart of any conflict.

LEGENDARY FIEND

The mere sight of this horrific demon drives most opponents insane!

DUELING LEGEND QUESTION # 18

WHICH BLOND BOY BULLIED YUGI BEFORE BEFRIENDING HIM?

ODION AND HIS MONSTER

Odion was adopted by Marik and Ishizu's parents and was the heir to the role of tombkeeper of the Pharaoh, until Marik was born. He will stand by Marik through thick and thin. However, little does Marik know that the mark on Odion's face suppresses the greater evil that resides within Marik's heart, so when Odion falls unconscious after a duel, the evil can no longer be repressed. . . .

EMBODIMENT OF APOPHIS

Embodiment of Apophis is a special type of monster — it's both a trap and a monster!

MYSTICAL BEAST SERKET

This monstrosity traps opponents in its giant claws and quickly eats them to gain power in a ferocious feeding frenzy!

MONSTER QUESTION # 18

67

WHICH ODION MONSTER FEASTS ON ITS OPPONENT'S MONSTERS TO GROW IN STRENGTH? ● ● ● ● ●

Ishizu Ishtar

Ishizu Ishtar is Marik's sister and the tombkeeper of the Pharaoh. With her Millennium Necklace, she is able to foresee future events. In order to save Marik from the evil that lurks within his soul, she gives Kaiba the Egyptian God Card, Obelisk the Tormentor, to start the Battle City Tournament and draw Marik out. She will stop at nothing to rescue Marik, even if it means risking everything she has.

MILLENNIUM NECKLACE

DUELING LEGEND QUESTION # 19

WHO INVENTED DUEL MONSTERS?

UMBRA AND LUMIS AND THEIR MONSTER

Marik's dueling duo, Umbra and Lumis, may seem like polar opposites: Umbra is tall, Lumis is short; Umbra has a shadow mask, Lumis has a light mask. However, when they work together, they can break up their opposing team's teamwork. During Battle City, they made even the great duelists Yugi and Kaiba suffer!

MASKED BEAST DES GUARDIUS

Much like its owners, this monster wears masks hiding its three faces of evil! However, nothing can mask its strength, for it's even more powerful than Blue-Eyes White Dragon!

ARKANA AND HIS MONSTERS

Once a great magician, Arkana suffered a freak accident that left his face scarred forever. However, the greatest scar was to his heart when his assistant, who was also his love, left him. Now Arkana is a magician duelist who duels with his own Dark Magician!

DOLL OF DEMISE

Always the performer, Arkana unleashes his own twisted version of a ventriloquist's dummy. However, there's nothing funny about this doll's performance.

STRINGS

This mime doesn't speak softly and carry a big stick — he doesn't speak at all! While under Marik's control, Strings nearly defeated Yugi by using one of the Egyptian God Monsters, Slifer the Sky Dragon!

DARK MAGICIAN OF ARKANA

Arkana has his own Dark Magician to rival Yugi's Dark Magician! However, Yugi's faith in his Dark Magician is greater than Arkana's in his, which was the key to Yugi's victory!

MONSTER QUESTION # 19

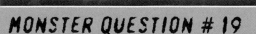

WHO IS THE APPRENTICE TO THE DARK MAGICIAN? ● ● ● ● ● ● ● ● ● ● ●

GOZABURO KAIBA AND HIS MONSTER

Gozaburo adopted Seto and Mokuba from the orphanage after Seto defeated Gozaburo in a chess match. Gozaburo was president of KaibaCorp, a company that made weapons of war. Seto wanted to change the company from one that made tanks to one that made games for kids, but Gozaburo would have none of that. Therefore, Seto initiated a hostile takeover and took KaibaCorp away from Gozaburo, filling Gozaburo with anger and rage. He uploaded his consciousness into a cyberworld, where he planned to lock Seto and Yugi in virtual reality forever!

EXODIA NECROSS

Exodia Necross looks just like Exodia the Forbidden One, except it is much more sinister, for it is invulnerable to monsters, spells, and traps! It's practically invincible!

DARTZ AND HIS MONSTER

Dartz was the king of Atlantis ten thousand years ago, so why is he alive today? That is one of the many mysteries surrounding the sinister Dartz. What little that is known about him is that he uses a mystical stone known as the Orichalcos to capture souls. With every soul captured, he stockpiles strength to revive Grand Dragon Leviathan. When Grand Dragon Leviathan is resurrected, he will be able to destroy the world and restart history!

GRAND DRAGON LEVIATHAN

This gargantuan beast dwarfs even the Egyptian God Monsters in size, for it is literally hundreds of feet long! This terror brought the fall of Atlantis ten millennia ago, and it intends to finish the job and destroy the world again!

RAFAEL

Rafael's history is full of tragedy. When he was on a cruise as a child, a huge monster sank his ship, separating him from his family. Luckily, he washed ashore on an isolated island in the middle of the ocean — but he was all alone. Until he was rescued many years later, his only companions were his guardian monster cards. Dartz recruited him, and Rafael duels using the guardian monsters that protected him many years ago.

The Legendary Dragons

The three Legendary Dragons — Timaeus, Critias, and Hermos — are the protectors of the domain of monsters. They stopped Dartz and Grand Dragon Leviathan from destroying the world ten millennia ago and put the Leviathan to sleep. However, Grand Dragon Leviathan has started to reawaken, so the Legendary Dragons must stop it one more time! However, this time they need the help of three legendary duelists to stop the world from being annihilated!

TIMAEUS

Yugi was brought to the domain of monsters by Dark Magician Girl to free Timaeus from its crystalline prison! Together, they're ready to stop Dartz from taking over the world again, for Timaeus can combine with other monsters to form powerful new monsters, especially when Timaeus combines with Dark Magician Girl to form Dark Magician Girl the Dragon Knight!

But Timaeus is an honorable dragon — Yugi must be worthy to earn Timaeus's help. Therefore, when Yugi betrays his monsters in his duel against Rafael, Timaeus refuses to help Yugi! Yugi has to regain Timaeus's trust, but that's easier said than done!

CRITIAS

After ten thousand years, the world needs the Legendary Dragons' help, and Critias has answered the call! It teams up with Kaiba, one of the three chosen legendary duelists! Critias combines with a monster and a trap to form a new monster that has the advantages of both a trap and a monster!

HERMOS

Hermos has chosen Joey to be the legendary duelist who can use its powers and abilities! Hermos combines with Time Wizard to form Time Magic Hammer, a winged mallet that can teleport opponents into the future and away from the field of battle! Hermos also joined with Rocket Warrior to transform into Rocket Hermos Cannon, a brutal blaster that can annihilate all its enemies!

Egyptian God Cards

While researching ancient carvings in Egypt, Pegasus learned about the most powerful creatures in history—the three Egyptian God Monsters: Slifer the Sky Dragon, Obelisk the Tormentor, and The Winged Dragon of Ra. Based on his findings, Pegasus created the Egyptian God Cards, but even *he* was scared of the enormous power of these cards. Therefore, he locked them away, hoping that no one would find them. Unfortunately, they were found. . . .

Now that they are in the open, everyone wants the Egyptian God Cards because they are the most powerful cards in all of Duel Monsters! However, for Yugi, there is more to these cards than power. Legend speaks that the Egyptian God Cards are one of the keys to unlocking the Pharaoh's past. . . .

SLIFER THE SKY DRAGON

Yugi's Slifer the Sky Dragon grows in strength for every card in his hand. Just as devastating is its second top mouth that attacks monsters the instant they're summoned! It's a one-dragon army of destruction!

OBELISK THE TORMENTOR

As other monsters are offered to Kaiba's Obelisk the Tormentor, it gains greater and greater strength until its power is infinite! With infinite power comes infinite victory!

THE WINGED DRAGON OF RA

Marik's The Winged Dragon of Ra has multiple abilities and forms, and each one is devastating! Not just anyone can use this Egyptian God Monster, however, for the card is written in ancient Egyptian writing.

THE WINGED DRAGON OF RA – SPHERE FORM

In Marik's duel against Mai, Mai was able to take control of The Winged Dragon of Ra! Unfortunately, the text on the card was written in ancient Egyptian writing, so she didn't know how to read it and use the card! The Winged Dragon of Ra remained in its Sphere Form and refused to listen to her!

THE WINGED DRAGON OF RA – EGYPTIAN GOD PHOENIX

Like the phoenix that rises from the dead, The Winged Dragon of Ra emerges from the graveyard as the Egyptian God Phoenix! Surrounded in flames, it unleashes a searing attack that engulfs its opponent in fire!

Monster Match!

How well do you know your duelists? Draw a line across the page that matches each legendary duelist to his or her monster!

WHICH MONSTER IS MADE OUT OF THREE MAGNETIC WARRIORS? • • • • • • • •

IT TAKES A KEEN EYE TO BECOME A DUELING LEGEND! SEE HOW MANY
LEGENDARY DUELISTS YOU CAN FIND HIDDEN IN THE LETTERS BELOW!

Yugi	Pegasus	Bakura	Bonz	Kaiba	Rafael
Mai	Marik	Odion	PaniK	Umbra	Paradox
Joey	Arkana	Weevil	Dartz	Lumis	

```
B W E E V I L L L C
B A F U Z K E R U T
J K K T M A I X M G
K O R U F B K T I P
O A E A R I R T S E
D P R Y F A F A P G
I N A A R K A N A A
O T S R K P I R N S
N P W I A G B K I U
P K R G U D L O K S
R A N Y R C O X N F
M K A I B A M X W Z
```

DUELING LEGEND QUESTION # 20

WHO POSSESSES THE MILLENNIUM PUZZLE?

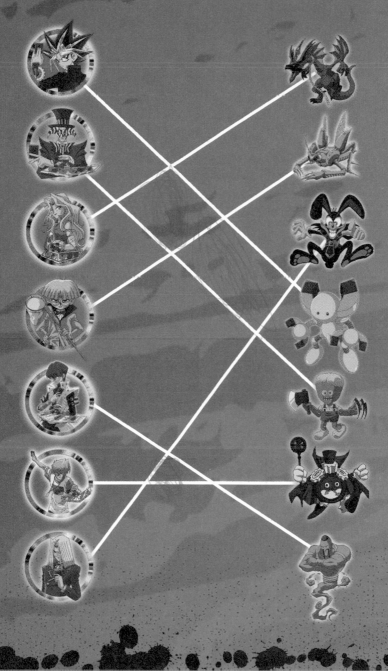

DUELING LEGENDS ANSWERS

1. PARADOX BROTHERS (PAGE 10)
2. ARKANA (PAGE 12)
3. SETO KAIBA (PAGE 16)
4. BAKURA (PAGE 20)
5. REX RAPTOR (PAGE 26)
6. DARTZ (PAGE 28)
7. BONZ (PAGE 32)
8. MAXIMILLION PEGASUS (PAGE 36)
9. WEEVIL UNDERWOOD (PAGE 40)
10. MARIK ISHTAR (PAGE 42)
11. JOEY WHEELER (PAGE 46)
12. ISHIZU ISHTAR (PAGE 48)
13. MAKO TSUNAMI (PAGE 54)
14. MAI VALENTINE (PAGE 58)
15. MAXIMILLION PEGASUS (PAGE 60)
16. MAXIMILLION PEGASUS (PAGE 62)
17. ODION (PAGE 64)
18. JOEY WHEELER (PAGE 66)
19. MAXIMILLION PEGASUS (PAGE 68)
20. YUGI (PAGE 78)

MONSTER ANSWERS

1. EXODIA THE FORBIDDEN ONE (PAGE 9)
2. THE LEGENDARY FISHERMAN (PAGE 11)
3. OBELISK THE TORMENTOR (PAGE 15)
4. EXODIA NECROSS (PAGE 19)
5. EMBODIMENT OF APOPHIS (PAGE 23)
6. CRITIAS (PAGE 29)
7. MASKED BEAST DES GARDIUS (PAGE 31)
8. THE WINGED DRAGON OF RA (PAGE 35)
9. TOON MERMAID (PAGE 39)
10. HARPIE'S PET DRAGON (PAGE 43)
11. XYZ-DRAGON CANNON (PAGE 45)
12. DRILLAGO (PAGE 49)
13. BLUE-EYES ULTIMATE DRAGON (PAGE 51)
14. JINZO (PAGE 59)
15. TIME WIZARD (PAGE 61)
16. SLIFER THE SKY DRAGON (PAGE 63)
17. GAIA THE FIERCE KNIGHT (PAGE 65)
18. MYSTICAL BEAST SERKET (PAGE 67)
19. DARK MAGICIAN GIRL (PAGE 69)
20. VALKYRION THE MAGNA WARRIOR (PAGE 77)

ANSWERS FOR PAGE 78

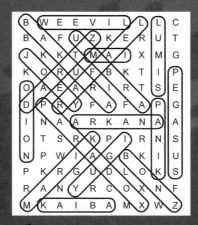